Number World

NUMBERS AT SCHOOL

Written by
Noah Leatherland

KidHaven
PUBLISHING

Published in 2024 by
KidHaven Publishing, an Imprint of Greenhaven Publishing, LLC
2544 Clinton St., Buffalo, NY 14224

© 2023 BookLife Publishing Ltd.

Written by: Noah Leatherland
Edited by: Rebecca Phillips-Bartlett
Designed by: Ker Ker Lee

Image Credits
All images are courtesy of Shutterstock.com, unless otherwise specified—
with thanks to Getty Images, Thinkstock Photo ,and iStockphoto.
Cover – frikota, MoreMass, Belozersky, Lomonovskyi, Shannon Marie Baldwin.
Internals – Yindee, ClassicVector, Sonium art, Rvector, Toywork, Microba Grandioza, Belozersky,
vector_brothers, Neliakott, Colorfuel Studio, MariVolkoff, Lara Lara, Biscotto Design, Irina Danyliuk

Cataloging-in-Publication Data

Names: Leatherland, Noah.
Title: Numbers at school / Noah Leatherland.
Description: Buffalo, New York : KidHaven Publishing, 2024. | Series: Number world
Identifiers: ISBN 9781534546325 (pbk.) | ISBN 9781534546332 (library bound) | ISBN 9781534546349 (ebook)
Subjects: LCSH: Counting--Juvenile literature. | Schools--Juvenile literature. |
School environment--Juvenile literature.
Classification: LCC QA113.L438 2024 | DDC 513.2'11--dc23

Manufactured in the United States of America

CPSIA compliance information: Batch #CW24KH: For further information contact Greenhaven Publishing LLC at 1-844-317-7404.

Please visit our website, www.greenhavenpublishing.com.
For a free color catalog of all our high-quality books, call toll free 1-844-317-7404 or fax 1-844-317-7405.

Find us on 🅵 🅸

4

I can see one teacher.

1

5

6

I can see **two** rulers.

I can see three books.

4

I can see four pens.

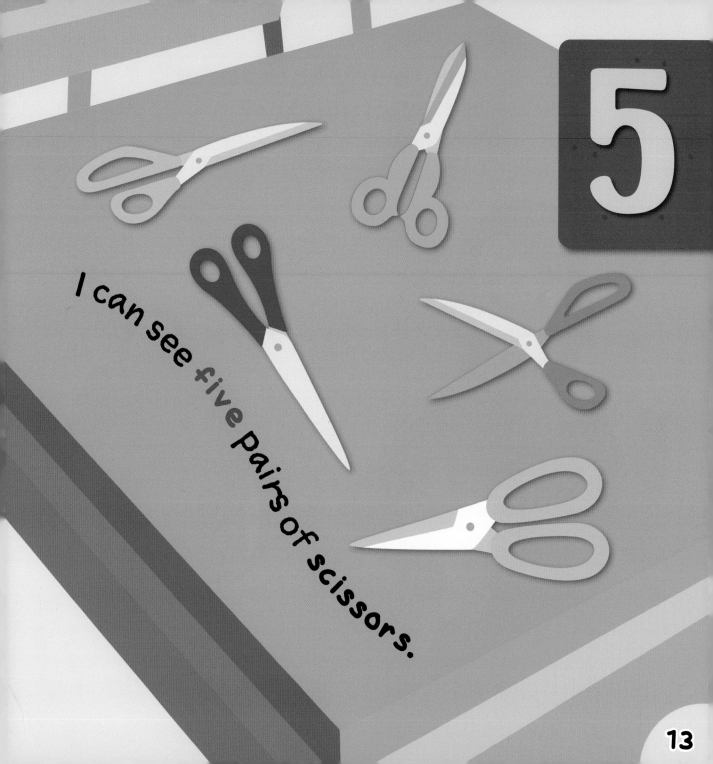

I can see five pairs of scissors.

I can see **six** backpacks.

I can see seven glue sticks.

I can see eight lunch boxes.

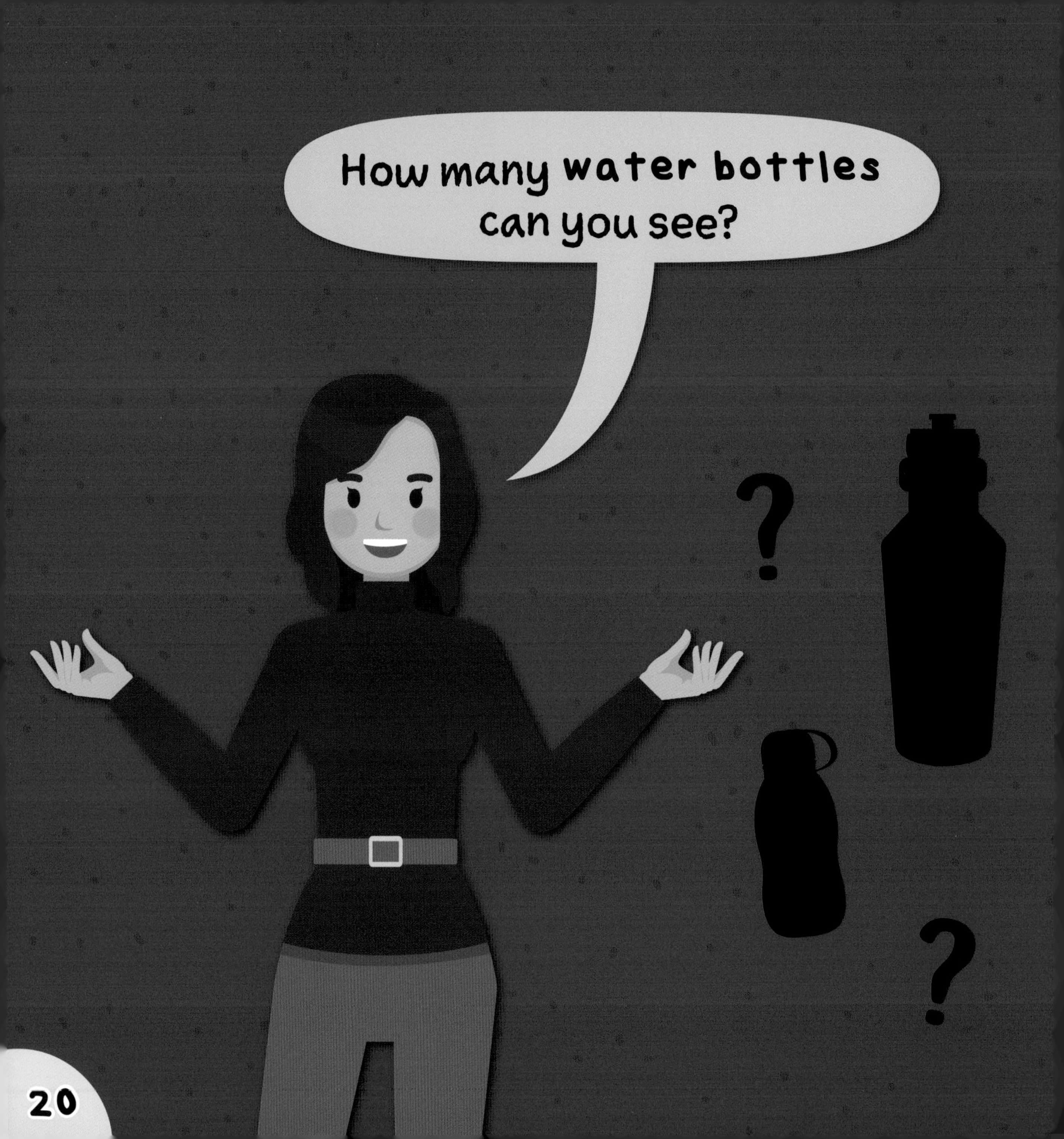
How many water bottles can you see?

I can see nine water bottles.

9

I can see ten students.

10

We can see a lot at school!

one teacher

two rulers

three books

four pens

five pairs of scissors

six backpacks

seven glue sticks

eight lunch boxes

nine water bottles

ten students